MEET DWYANE WADE

Basketball's Rising Star

John Smithwick

Published in 2007 by The Rosen Publishing Group, Inc.
29 East 21st Street, New York, NY 10010

First Edition

Editor: Jennifer Way
Book Design: Greg Tucker
Photo Researcher: Sam Cha

Photo Credits: Cover, p. 1 © Jim McIsaac/Getty Images; p. 4 © Al Bello/Getty Images; pp. 7, 16 © Lisa Blumenfeld/Getty Images; p. 8 © Doug Benc/Getty Images; pp. 9, 15, 22, 30 © Doug Pensinger/Getty Images; pp. 11, 13 © Elsa/Getty Images; p. 12 © Jonathan Daniel/Getty Images; p. 17 © Stephen Dunn/Getty Images; p. 18 © Stuart Hannagan/Getty Images; p. 20 © Jed Jacobsohn/Getty Images; p. 23 © Brian Bahr/Getty Images; p. 25 © Kevin Winter/Getty Images; p. 26 © Frazer Harrison/Getty Images; p. 28 © Robert Sullivan/AFP/Getty Images; p. 29 © Ronald Martinez/Getty Images.

Library of Congress Cataloging-in-Publication Data

Smithwick, John.
    Meet Dwyane Wade : basketball's rising star / John Smithwick. — 1st ed.
        p. cm. — (All-star players)
    Includes index.
    ISBN-13: 978-1-4042-3639-4 (library binding)
    ISBN-10: 1-4042-3639-2 (library binding)
    1. Wade, Dwyane, 1982– —Juvenile literature. 2. Basketball players—United States—Biography—Juvenile literature. I. Title. II. Series.

    GV884.W23S64 2007
    796.323092—dc22
    [B]

                                    2006022369

Manufactured in the United States of America

Contents

Dwyane Wade (center) is one of the most exciting basketball players in the NBA. He is excellent at many different basketball skills.

Dwyane Wade is one of the hardest-working and most **athletic** basketball players in the NBA. Dwyane Wade, whose teammates nicknamed him "Flash," is one of the fastest and most **agile** guards in the NBA. He is basketball's newest superstar.

Wade is a guard for the Miami Heat. Each basketball team has two guards. A guard's job is basically to move the ball. Guards must be good at every part of basketball. They must be good shooters and be able to make baskets from anywhere on the court. They must be good passers, in order to help teammates score. They also must be strong **defensive** players. Wade is all of these things and more.

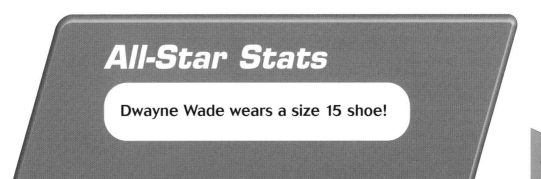

All-Star Stats

Dwayne Wade wears a size 15 shoe!

Dwyane Wade was born in Chicago, Illinois. His parents, Dwyane Sr. and Jolinda, divorced when he was very young. After the divorce Wade's parents remained on friendly terms. This allowed Dwyane and his sister, Tragil, to spend lots of time with each parent. Dwyane and Tragil had a close bond. To this day Wade considers his sister his best friend.

Dwyane Sr. had a love for basketball. He coached a team of young players at a local gym. When Dwyane was old enough to play, he joined the team and fell in love with basketball.

Dwyane also played football. While playing in high school, he actually showed more talent on

All-Star Stats

Wade enjoys reading. It is one of his favorite pastimes.

Here is Wade making a slam dunk against the Los Angeles Lakers' Smush Parker.

the football field than he did on the basketball court. Dwyane, however, preferred basketball. He knew that he needed to improve his basketball skills if he wanted to make the team. Dwyane practiced and worked out, **determined** to turn himself into a basketball player. The hard work paid off, and by Dwyane's last

Dwyane worked hard to become a better player. Here he is making a layup with the Miami Heat in 2005.

year of high school, he could play any position on the court. He averaged 20.7 points a game, which was an excellent average for a high-school player.

One of the reasons Dwyane is considered a great player is because he is able to play many different positions on the court. He is a guard for the Miami Heat.

In spite of Wade's outstanding career in high-school basketball, he did not receive the **scholarship** offers that most talented young athletes get. These scholarships pay for the athlete's education in full. The college basketball coaches **underestimated** Wade. It was not the last time that would happen.

One college was interested in Wade but not interested enough to offer him a full basketball scholarship. Marquette University, in Milwaukee, Wisconsin, offered Wade a scholarship that covered part of his education. He was determined to prove that he belonged on a top college basketball team. During his freshman year, Wade practiced with the team, but he was not allowed to join them for games. He could not travel with the team for away games. He did not even get to wear a uniform.

In his time at Marquette University, Wade led his team in points and even set a school record in scoring.

Wade made the most of this situation. Marquette's coach, Tom Crean, told Wade to sit beside him during all the home games. Wade learned a lot about basketball **strategy** from Crean during those games.

Wade put this knowledge to use when he suited up with the team in his sophomore, or second, year. Wade led Marquette in points,

Here is Wade scoring against Missouri in the 2003 NCAA Tournament.

rebounds, assists, and steals. He also set a school record when he scored 571 points in one season.

Wade did even better in his junior year. He led Marquette to the Final Four in the NCAA **tournament**. Along the way Wade became the third player in tournament history to make a triple-double. This means he had double digits in points, rebounds, and assists. Wade's excellent junior year would get him noticed by NBA scouts.

Wade is cutting his piece of net after Marquette won the Midwest Regional NCAA Tournament. Teammates often take turns cutting down their home-court net after a winning season.

Wade's junior year was so successful that NBA coaches and scouts started paying close attention to him. It became clear that he was ready to play **professional** basketball.

Wade had married his high-school sweetheart, Siohvaughn, and had a son, Zaire, in 2002. Having a family to support, in addition to the growing attention from NBA scouts, helped Wade decide to skip his last year of college to make millions of dollars in the NBA.

Wade entered the 2003 NBA **Draft**. The draft is the system the NBA uses to place new players with teams. Only the teams with the worst records get to pick the first-round players from the **lottery**. This system makes sure that the best players go to teams that need their talent.

The 2003 draft showcased a lot of talent. High-school basketball star LeBron James drew most of the attention. He was the first player picked.

Wade (left) is playing against Larry Hughes of the Washington Wizards during Wade's first NBA season.

This is Wade (left) guarding Kobe Bryant of the Los Angeles Lakers.

Wade was chosen fifth, by the Miami Heat. Once again he had been underestimated.

The Heat struggled during Wade's first season. To make matters worse, Wade hurt his wrist and missed nearly a month of play. Once again Wade made the most of his time on the bench. He paid attention to the coaches and learned strategy.

When Wade got back on the court, he and the Heat made it to the play-offs. Considering the team's shaky start to the season, this was quite an accomplishment.

Miami ended up losing to the Indiana Pacers, but Wade was not discouraged. His rookie season had been a huge success.

Wade was proud of how well he and his team played during his rookie season, which was 2003–2004.

17

The U.S. team won the bronze
medal in the 2004 Olympics. Here
is Wade taking a shot during one
of the Dream Team's games.

The 2004 Olympics

In 2004, Wade was selected to represent the United States as part of the men's Olympic basketball team in Athens, Greece. Nicknamed the "Dream Team," the U.S. men's basketball team is usually favored to win the gold **medal**. No other country produces so many talented basketball players. Therefore, it was a huge letdown when the United States won the third-place bronze medal and not the first-place gold medal.

Because they were young players, Wade and LeBron James saw limited playing time in the Olympics. Today they are considered to be two of the best players in the NBA. It is possible that the U.S. team would have done better had they played more.

Shaquille O'Neal (right) joined the
Heat in 2004. He and Wade
have become friends.

Wade's Second Season

The Miami Heat owners realized they needed another star player to help Wade. They wanted an experienced player who could act as his **mentor**. Fortunately, one of the greatest basketball players of all time, Shaquille O'Neal, of the Los Angeles Lakers, was looking for a new team.

O'Neal, nicknamed "Shaq," quickly became friends with Wade. He was astonished by Wade's **versatility**. Wade could make himself useful to the team in any situation. He would often turn the tide of a game simply by being in the right place at the right time. Shaq gave Wade a nickname of his own, calling him Flash for his ability to be everywhere at once. Soon the rest of the Heat began calling Wade by this nickname.

O'Neal proved to be just what Wade and the Heat needed to improve. They became the best

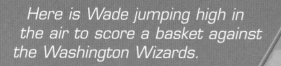

Here is Wade jumping high in the air to score a basket against the Washington Wizards.

team in the Eastern **Conference** in the 2004–2005 season. Wade even recorded a triple-double against the Detroit Pistons.

Miami made the play-offs for the second year in a row. They beat the New Jersey Nets with a clean sweep. They went on to sweep their next challenger, the Washington Wizards, as well. In each of these series of games, Wade averaged more than 30 points a game. Wade's outstanding second season ended when Miami lost to the Detroit Pistons. Wade finished the 2004–2005 season as one of the most talented players in the game. His next season would prove to be his best yet and would make history.

Basketball is not the only thing in Wade's life. The highlight of his life is not a basketball accomplishment. It is the birth of his son, Zaire. He is also a loving husband to his wife, Siohvaughn.

Wade has many interests off the court. His Miami Heat uniform shirt was a top seller during the 2005–2006 season. He became a model for the Sean John clothing line by Sean "Diddy" Combs. In 2005, *People* magazine placed him on its annual 50 Most Beautiful People list. Converse created a line of shoes named after Wade.

Wade **donates** 10 percent of his salary to his hometown church in Chicago. He also encourages children to read. Wade's favorite book is Jane Austen's *Pride and Prejudice*. The book is about

Wade is known for his personal style. Here he is at the 2005 ESPY Awards, at which he won as the Best Breakthrough Athlete.

All-Star Stats

In 2006, *GQ* magazine called Wade the best-dressed player in the NBA.

people overcoming **stereotypes**, and Wade thinks everyone should read it.

Wade majored in **broadcasting** at Marquette. He got good grades, and he hopes to put these skills to use and talk about basketball on TV when he retires from the NBA.

Besides fashion Wade's other loves include his family, his church, and reading.

MVP and Beyond

The 2005–2006 season proved to be Wade's best yet. While averaging more than 27 points a game, he led the Heat to the play-offs for the third year in a row. Even though he had caught the flu, Wade played six great games in the Eastern Conference Finals and helped Miami beat the Detroit Pistons.

Miami advanced to face the Dallas Mavericks in the 2006 NBA Championship. Things looked bad when the Heat lost the first two games. Wade responded by leading Miami to win the next four games. The Heat won their first championship. Wade scored a total of 157 points in the four Miami wins and was named Most Valuable Player, or MVP, of the series. His play earned comparisons

Wade was the top choice for the MVP after his performance in the 2006 NBA Finals.

with Michael Jordan, the greatest basketball player in history. Wade is young and has many years of basketball left to play. It is certain that he will never be underestimated again!

This is the Heat celebrating their 2006 NBA Finals win.

Stat Sheet

Height: 6'4" (1.9 m)
Weight: 212 pounds (96 kg)
Team: Miami Heat
Uniform Number: 3
Date of Birth: January 17, 1982
Years in NBA: 3

2005–2006 Season Stats

Points per Game	Rebounds per Game	Assists per Game	Total Points
27.2	5.7	6.7	2,040

NBA Career Stats as of Summer 2006

Points per Game	Rebounds per Game	Assists per Game	Total Points
22.9	5	6.1	4,885

Glossary

agile (A-jul) Able to move easily and gracefully.

athletic (ath-LEH-tik) Having ability and training in sports and exercises of strength.

broadcasting (BROD-kast-ing) Working in radio and TV.

conference (KON-frens) A grouping of sports teams.

defensive (DEE-fent-siv) Playing in a position that tries to stop the other team from scoring.

determined (dih-TER-mind) Firm in purpose.

donates (DOH-nayts) Gives money or help.

draft (DRAFT) The selection of people for a special purpose.

lottery (LAH-tuh-ree) The drawing of lots used to decide something. Lots are objects used as counters in a lottery.

medal (MEH-dul) A small, round piece of metal that is given as a prize.

mentor (MEN-tor) A trusted guide or teacher.

professional (pruh-FESH-nul) Paid to do something.

scholarship (SKAH-ler-ship) Money given to someone to pay for school.

stereotypes (STER-ee-uh-typs) Images, usually bad, about a person or a group.

strategy (STRA-tuh-jee) The planning and directing of movements on the field.

tournament (TOR-nuh-ment) A contest to see who wins the most games.

underestimated (un-dur-ES-tih-mayt-ed) Placed too low a value on.

versatility (ver-suh-TIH-luh-tee) The ability to do many different things well.

Index

Web Sites

Due to the changing nature of Internet links, PowerKids Press has developed an online list of Web sites related to the subject of this book. This site is updated regularly. Please use this link to access the list:

www.powerkidslinks.com/asp/dwyane/